This book belongs to

_____

This book is dedicated to my children - Mikey, Kobe, and Jojo.

Copyright © 2025 Grow Grit Press LLC. All rights reserved. No part of this book may be reproduced in any form without permission in writing from the publisher. Please send bulk order requests to info@ninjalifehacks.tv

Paperback ISBN: 979-8-89614-118-1
Hardcover ISBN: 979-8-89614-120-4
eBook ISBN: 979-8-89614-119-8

Printed and bound in the USA.
NinjaLifeHacks.tv

Ninja Life Hacks®
by Mary Nhin

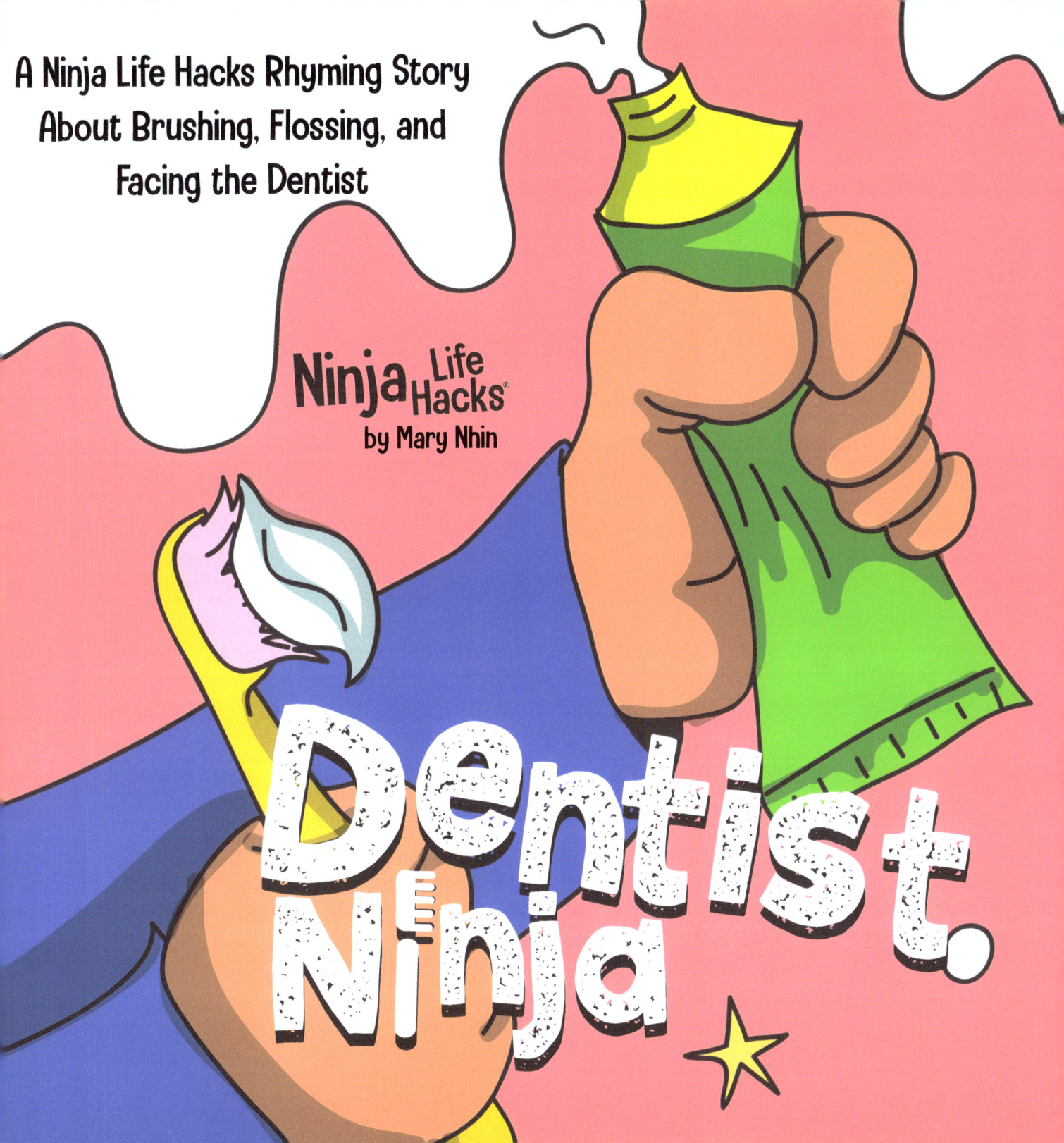

Hi, I'm Dentist Ninja, it's true,
I clean, I check, and teach what to do.
When teeth get gunky or gums turn red,
I'm the one who helps instead!

My first checkup, I was tense.
The dentist chair felt so intense!
But then I learned it's not so bad.
In fact, that visit made me glad!

They counted teeth, they took a peek,
They even made my molars squeak!
They told me, "Ninja, you're doing great!"
And gave me stickers near the gate.

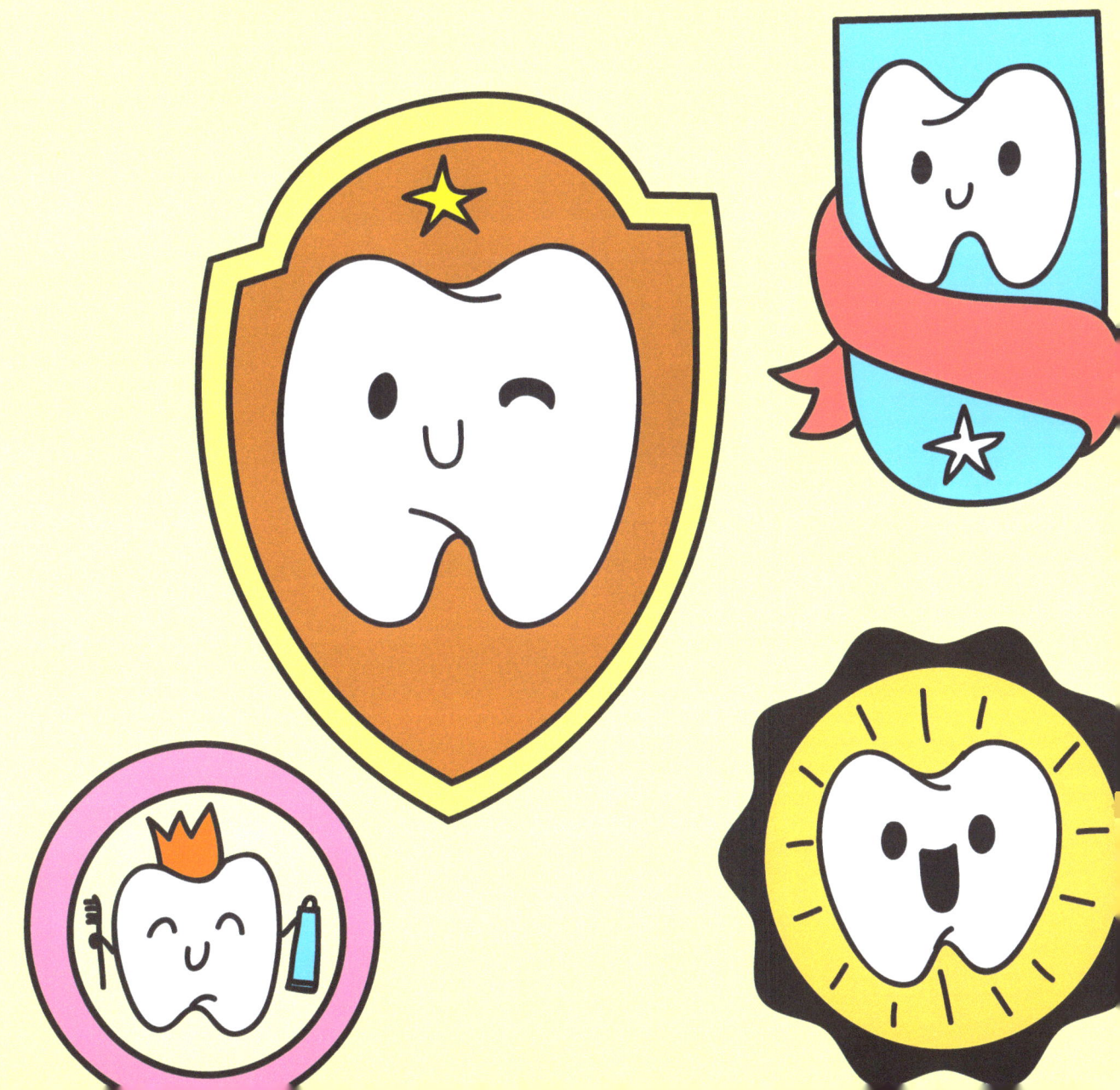

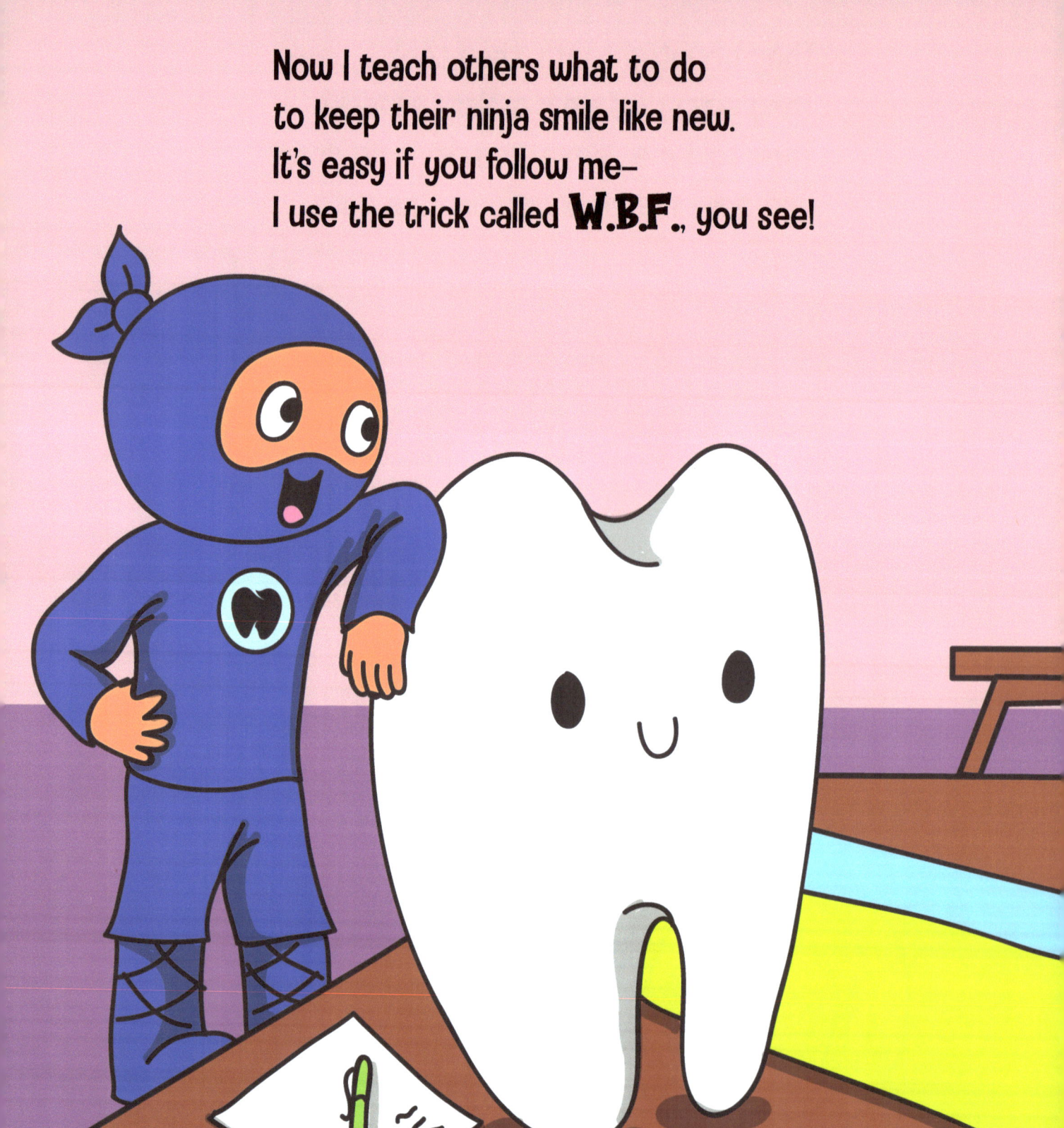

B is for **Brushing**, morning and night,
with gentle circles, not too tight.
Two minutes long, from cheek to cheek–
My ninja teeth stay fresh all week!

Some kids worry, some kids hide.
But going to the dentist? I smile wide!
It shows I care and want to grow—
because checkups help my smile glow!

My toothbrush wears a ninja mask.
My floss does flips—it's up to the task!
My cup of water bows with grace,
to keep me smiling face to face.

Now I go with ninja pride,
I hop into the chair like it's a ride!
Because brave ninjas, yes it's true,
take care of teeth like champions do.

Be proud of every ninja tooth.
Your habits now will show your truth.
Just follow **W.B.F.** today...
And you'll keep that ninja plaque away!

NINJA SMILE HALL OF FAME

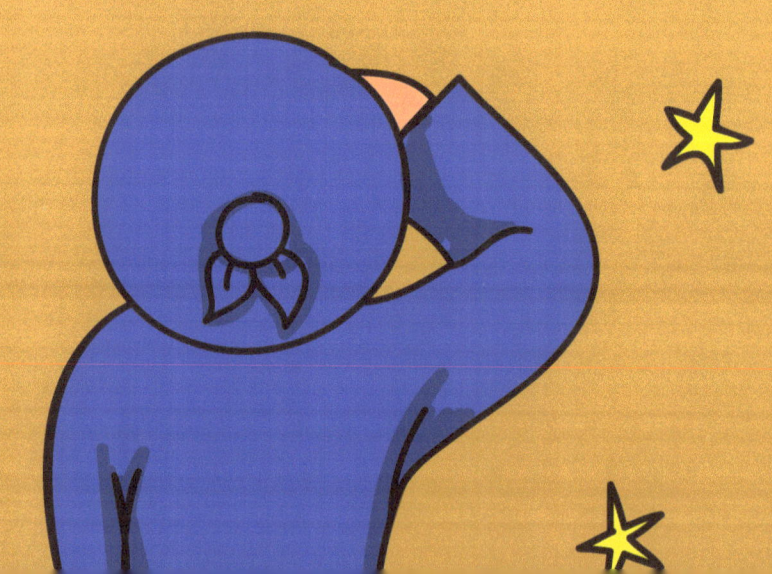

"BRUSH LiKE A NiNJA" SONG
(Sing to the tune of "Twinkle, Twinkle, Little Star")

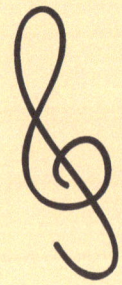

Brush your teeth from left to right,
Morning, evening, day and night.
Up and down and round you go,
Make those ninja pearlies glow!
Don't forget to floss in style—
Clean between each ninja smile!

Check out the fun Dentist Ninja lesson plans at ninjalifehacks.tv

I love to hear from my readers. Email me your feedback or thoughts on what my next story should be at info@ninjalifehacks.tv   Yours truly, Mary

 @marynhin   @officialninjalifehacks
#NinjaLifeHacks

 Mary Nhin   Ninja Life Hacks

 Ninja Life Hacks

 @officialninjalifehacks

www.ingramcontent.com/pod-product-compliance
Lightning Source LLC
LaVergne TN
LVHW070436070526
838199LV00015B/524